Sugar Too Sweet

Sugar Too Sweet

by

Alexandra Vincent

ISBN: 9798218182977

Book design & layout by Alexandra Vincent

First printing edition, 2023.

Alexandra Vincent
@alexandra.j.vincent
alexandrajvincent.com

Contents

Golden Era

Mad Honey

Bittersweet

Introduction

Not all stories are easy to tell. I'm sure many of you have chapters in your life; that affect you deeply. My hope with this collection is to bring forth connection. We all go through love and loss at some point in our lives. Each situation may be a bit different, but we all fight through the grief, healing, reflection, and acceptance that follows.

I wrote *Sugar Too Sweet*; so we can take on those concepts together. We can feel happy, sad, angry, numb, and confused. But hopeful still.

Golden Era

Part One

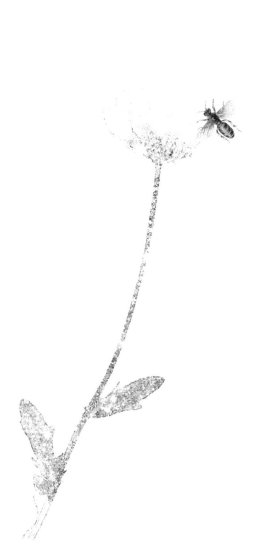

I told you one day I would write a book about you.

Here it is.

You were a pure cup of sunshine.

From the very first sip, you had me hooked.

Sugar Too Sweet

Love
be it passion so deep
rooted at the center
seeping through the barks of the trees
dripping to your lips
a soft sweet kiss.

You gave me a blush
no one has seen before
plump rosy cheeks
you say you love and adore.

Sugar Too Sweet

The summer rain
showers falling from above
light crossing through every drop

that was you

with cotton-candy skies
as the perfect back drop
admitting ambiguity and radiancy.

I truly admire you
dancing in the hues
of gold

how special it is
to be with
the twin flame of the sun.

Sugar Too Sweet

Green is my favorite color
you said
as two opal cupid stones
met
my jungle-green wastelands.

I never experienced such a rush
the sweet serendipity
swallowed me up
and brought me to the warmest
place.

Sugar Too Sweet

Sugar

Late night talks and jazzy tunes
to Norah's voice, we sway to the blues
toes to toes, nose to nose
I've got "the nearness of you"

stormy clouds
hung over your crystal waters
with drunken highs
we explored our wonders

smoke clouds and ash
land at our feet
crisp fall air is coming
how bittersweet

and the blueberry pie
sugar so nice
time stopped with
you and I.

We felt like one in many ways.

Sugar Too Sweet

At some point
we must have gotten lost
between *this is temporary*
and casting the weights at our feet
tying the heartstrings together
double-knotted, tight enough
that it would take two to undo.

Alexandra Vincent

I told the trees and their leaves
all the lakes and seas I got to meet
the moon and all the stars
I could see in our galaxy

I told them all about you.

Sugar Too Sweet

You opened the door
to a world I hadn't seen
oozing with sweet sunshine
and dare I say

a happier me.

Alexandra Vincent

Your love flooded in
like dappled light
pouring through the gaps of the leaves
at summer's sunrise

no foliage too plentiful
nor the buzzing of honeybees
that filled my mind in a swarm
could ever begin
to bring a lapse to your warmth.

Sugar Too Sweet

Blanketed by the midnight sky
a smokers rasp tickles my ears
I'm being tangled up
under your agonizing long stares
hypnotic jewels dazzling with the stars
in all shades of silver and blue
I could feel every part of me
falling for you.

Alexandra Vincent

My soul like a meadow
shifting with the seasons

from wild, green, and prosperous
to torched black weeds
waiting to breathe life
once again.

Sugar Too Sweet

You followed me in the dark
where my mind hid with cloudy stars
cloaked I was like the night
hidden with lock and key
but you searched high and low
every surface
trying to find me.

In my black-and-white world
I look at you
and see all gray
imperfect hidden gem
amongst all my castaways.

Sugar Too Sweet

Sentiment

With you the little things
felt significant
they grew to be more than life's fillers
in the gaps of mundane moments

they were like a breath of fresh air
and a blissful taste of sentiment
not a moment without you
could ever compare.

Talking for hours
and late into the night
becoming the keeper of my mind

you encouraged the dreamer in me
making me believe
I could conquer anything.

Sugar Too Sweet

Talking to brick walls was common
but you listened
tapped into every word I'd say
so of course, it took me by surprise
every time I tapered off
and you'd say

I'm still listening.

It's the honey in my lungs
a sticky suffocation
and the sweet surrender
to the face of a thrill
with the one
divine vixen.

Sugar Too Sweet

This love brought me to the highest high
my head was in the clouds
and I never imagined my feet
could grace the ground
she made me feel alive again
the dead girl inside me had risen.

Alexandra Vincent

I don't know if I want to do this
or what will come of it
your eyes hold mystery
and my body feels jittery

because

you won't give me time
to make up my mind
before I can say anything
your lips are on mine
and like that
the breath I needed is gone
the shirt on my back is gone
the moment I had to say
yes or no

is gone.

Sugar Too Sweet

Desire

How the desire plants in you over night
by the time the sun is set to rise
it's much too late to cultivate the roots
from wispy stems they take forbidden fruit
eaten with remorse
double-edged inclination has run its course.

Alexandra Vincent

Red rose and thorns
tatted to the skin
protecting your heart

what a foreshadowing moment in our story.

Sugar Too Sweet

Fate

Of course, I'd write our story
in watercolors
gliding whimsical and bright
canvas being crafted in many hues
as our love knows more than one color

but the shades begin to mix
bleeding down the page
slowly draining
and fading away
malignant fate stuck to our page

unfortunate for us
that was our love.

Mad Honey

Part Two

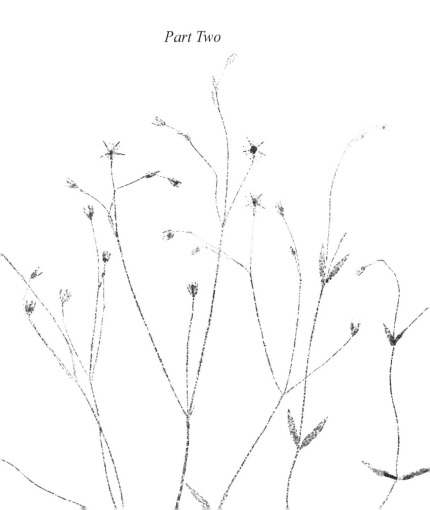

She was fire

she was ice

...classic Gemini

I could never help falling in love…

my soul only felt alive diving off the deep end.

Sugar Too Sweet

Rain in June

I thought we shared only sunny days ahead
but to my surprise
the cotton clouds
cast a bounty of raindrops down

tumbling to our nose
then settling between our toes
they sizzled on the scorched pavement
giving us a show

I saw the magic look in your eyes
and I wondered why
how you could not detest
the wreckage in the sky

you welcomed the rain
to our perfect summers day
as if you knew
it would soon go away.

Alexandra Vincent

My June
bleached blonde and sundrenched
a small season of running barefoot
through the grass at midsummer
fragrant flowers hit in the wind
the sweet smell of the short-lived
could have fooled anyone
into burning in the
heartbroken heatwaves.

Sugar Too Sweet

She's worldlier than me
decades older than me
living a life
I have yet to see.

Alexandra Vincent

A vivacious woman
is what you call yourself
offering such life and laughter
sometimes I wonder
if you are merely a contagion

or worse, a lifeline

that I so desperately need.

Sugar Too Sweet

She carved holes into me
digging for the skeletons
and all the words I kept from prying ears

why so surprised
when I pushed back
with the analytical thinking
you so adored
and tried to solve your mystery, too?

Alexandra Vincent

You cracked me open
cutting the seams
that I had violently shut
so long ago
each stitch being pulled
one by one
until there were none.

Sugar Too Sweet

You love how I'm shy
putting in the work to pry
me open
with a gentle touch or a knife

what will it be this time?

arms tied to the bed
safe word swimming in my head
pry me open
spread me open

maybe I should call red.

Alexandra Vincent

Honey Jar

Honey dripping down the walls
my thudding heart must hear the calls
from the charmed mouth that lingers still
coaxing the young who have no will
breadcrumbs of treats and company
the wicked lie buried behind the teeth

the sweet talk that graced my ears
has plagued my mind and hushed my fears
there was a hornet in my honey jar
but it's too late— we've gone too far
with this little game of *catch the mouse*
I find no haven in this little glass house.

Sugar Too Sweet

There were 30 years between me and you
and my gullible ways lead me astray
I couldn't see the fantasy you created
you found the perfect sugar plum
to play the part
I was just a character from the very start.

Young blood has been checked off your list.

I didn't think I would lose much by
being involved with you.

I didn't know life could do me dirty so many
times.

Alexandra Vincent

Maple Woods

The maple woods catch ahold of me
the dreamer
the wanderer
has been captured
now drowning in the sap
flooding from the trees
a gruesome sight
the sugar so sickening
toxins poison me

be it death by maple trees.

Sugar Too Sweet

I must have been sickly sweet
for you to devour me
and spit me out so quick.

I should have known
I should have realized
how every night
we pumped our bodies
with crown and coke
or weed
and tobacco smoke
my throat would burn
my stomach would churn
yet I never questioned
I never learned
how love couldn't thrive like that.

Sugar Too Sweet

You said it's not about me
so don't take it personally

if only I wasn't the pleaser of the people.

Alexandra Vincent

I lost my mind to unrequited love.

Sugar Too Sweet

Going through all her things
searching for the lies
the secrets
she keeps from me
is it maddening to say

I can't walk away.

My intentions were pure
I just needed more than anything
to secure
the love I thought she held for me

the locket of her heart
ticking, ticking, ticking
away inside

with tired eyes
I hold my place in line
with hope
I'll be the only one she'll have tonight.

Midnight Moments

My messy emotions
overtook me in the midnight hour
for the uninvited guest
you brought to bed
left me questioning what we ever had

these unfathomable moments
would soon get the best of me
bringing my mind to happenings
I wished I had seen

connecting the dots
was like chasing the
fireflies in the night sky
one would come
then another would pass me by.

Alexandra Vincnet

You hot glued pressed flowers
into tiny photo frames
how fragile they were
colors slipping away
lifeless body drained
and moved around
over and over again
uprooting them from home
to be forced into place
a grave in a frame
bestowed to all
coffin glass
nailed to a wall.

Sugar Too Sweet

You say you're sorry
but I don't think I believe you
I pace the floors all night
the voice in my head says
maybe we can start new
we can try again
but lies cut deep
and your love has been fading
again.

Alexandra Vincent

Bated
I don't think I can take it
being reeled in
with a soft summer kiss
lips on my skin
and your only wish
for our love to begin again.

*...but we went down this road
one too many times.*

Alexandra Vincent

My shelter was stripped
completely exposed
my sweet young soul was used
taken and returned
like an old school library book
missing pages and crumpled edges
and for love?

I don't think so.

Sugar Too Sweet

Lately I can't sleep at night
with these confusing thoughts on my mind
steal me away and light a fire inside
please call me home and turn on the lights.

Alexandra Vincent

We became strangers in the night
unknowingly
passing each other by.

Sugar Too Sweet

Another day down
another smoke out
another trail blazed
through our essence
tearing away piece by piece.

Disregard the possibility of heartache

I knew that would happen loving you…

loving anyone.

Our moments became fleeting
but my heart could not fathom

that our love wasn't timeless.

Alexandra Vincent

Time will tell
what the heart may not
silence will power
the final thought.

Sugar Too Sweet

Cold sheets at the start of the day
you must have slipped away
in the dead of night
you never said goodbye.

Alexandra Vincent

Slow goodbyes I think are worse
when we start drifting
further away every night
two sinking ships passing by
with no anchorage.

Sugar Too Sweet

Was I your sugar rush?

Was I candy between your teeth?

that tasty after dinner treat
and a bite ment
to be short and sweet

but never lasting.

Alexandra Vincent

Somehow, I just didn't know
how bad it really was
to be left and forgotten
though when you came trailing back
it made me forget all the past times
the lonely nights
spent wondering

do you miss me too?

Sugar Too Sweet

You left me with empty hands
nothing left to hold
you left me to explain
to every person we ever told
you left me with the dainty hoops
rose gold
you left me spinning in insanity
my heart growing cold
you left
you broke the mold.

Alexandra Vincent

Traces of dried petals
cover the floors
what a sentiment
to the love that was ignored
falling from the vase
being kicked to the corners
oh how they did try
so hard to warn her.

Sugar Too Sweet

Personal Reckoning

I ran barefoot
tearing up the roots beneath me
I knew walking in decaying woods
would be the gateway to my demise
never so wise I was
to chase what was never mine
our love lay wilting
in the center of the wreckage
yet I nurtured every black and brittle weed
breathing life into you
a soothing sweet delicacy
but the whispering winds told me
what my mind had feared
the darkness comes beckoning
I ran full force
into my own personal reckoning.

Bittersweet

Part Three

Sugar Too Sweet

I'll never forget my year being 22

it was golden
*   it was mad*
*   it was bittersweet.*

How am I too much…

yet not enough at the same time?

Sugar Too Sweet

Drain My Honey

You left me to tame your burning flames
embers dancing in the dark
in wait for a place to land
falling through the cracks of my hand

barren rooms falling in around me
the echoes of the inferno surround me
I can't withstand the heat
knowing you left me

a house or a home
my heart of a comb
near drained of all the honey
my pot of pure gold would soon run empty

so I'll sit in the pit of your burning attempt
to cover your tracks on the sticky sweet trail
you take my last gift of a shaking exhale
leave me for ash and bid me farewell.

Alexandra Vincent

I begged you to read between the lines
but I came to find
my book closed shut
not a word was read nor pondered about
I fear I asked too much
from a soul that never planned to give.

Sugar Too Sweet

Sweet Atlantis

Oh, sweet Atlantis
where have you been
I thought I saw you drifting by
did you go off the deep end

oh, sweet Atlantis
where are you now
I thought we could talk
but it seems you're not around

oh, sweet Atlantis
where did you go
I thought we could be together
but it seems I'm set alone

oh, sweet Atlantis
wherever you are
in the sky or the seas of blue
I'll wait right here for you.

What's a goodbye, without a goodbye?

Sugar Too Sweet

Hoping you would come back soon
the essence of time is lost in my mind
sat at the window for months on end
watched the seasons change
again and again.

Alexandra Vincent

Irredeemable mistakes
linger at the forefront
a loss from the aspiring intent
my false hope and shortcomings
fail to waver

so forever a lone heart will grieve.

Sugar Too Sweet

January & June

Everyone saw us as an unlikely pair
I was January; you were June
you had this delightful energy
like a flower at first bloom
and I was icy and oh so warry
that this serendipity
would come and go too soon.

and I wish my thoughts
were nothing more than just thoughts

but when the year had started new
and I was just January
with no June
I curled back up in the winter squall
and asked for any reason

why did you leave me last season?

Perfect Little Gem

Spring-scented secrets
invade my bleak winter
on the tip of my tongue
forgive and forget lingers

I was just emeralds in your eyes
a prize to be won
your perfect little gem
you would have till you're done

the lipstick stains
smudged on my little sundress
still blood red, how can I forget
the bitter mouth that made me a mess?

Sugar Too Sweet

She plucked all my petals
as if they will grow again
next season is uncertain
will I even grow a stem

for when May comes back around
I might not be the same
the April showers forget me
I heave in the drought that surrounds me

I have no rain
no sun to see
not one petal to grow
she took them all from me.

Sugar Plum

After years of being the keeper
holding on to all of the damage caused
I realized you were nothing more
then a trojan horse
weaseling your way in
with all your sugar-coated glory
only for me to find
a toxin filled inside
oozing with mad honey
on the quest to groom a sugar plum
and her lily-white frame.

Sugar Too Sweet

Sitting at the edge of the bed
dripping wet and half wrapped
in a towel much too small
the droplets falling to my toes
from my hair or eyes
I don't really know
I think if I don't move
maybe the world will follow
she will come to a stop
so I can finally swallow
the yearning ache
that keeps me awake
all day and night
will this earthly ball just come to a pause
may I have a moment of peace
from all the agony you caused?

She thought she was setting me free
but the truth was
she left my carcass on a dead-end street
dried out and torn
left for the birds.

Sugar Too Sweet

Losing you
was a bittersweet remedy
the driest pill I ever swallowed
with taunting aftershocks
that left me broken and hollow
but I'll thank the divine
because I'm finally on the mend
from a stirring sapphic romance.

You left me ages ago
yet your silhouette still stands
at the end of my bed
I pull the pillow over my head
but then I hear the humming begin
a melody you would think
but it's just sad torment
chills crawling up my spine
as hands of a ghost
trace against my skin
for a moment I'm there again
waiting for a rasping whisper

...goodnight.

Sugar Too Sweet

I often see you as the villain of our story
but other times reality centers me
and I remember the weakness
that would subtly cross those blue eyes
and I can only think you were a good human
simply having a hard time

and then the peace in me grows.

Your tired eyes
still find way to my mind
I recall how they wavered
so unsteady moving like the waves
shades of blue stirring up a storm
waiting for the rain to fall
unknown by all
the misery that swam so deeply in you.

Learning that we all live a sonder life...

was but the end creating a new beginning.

I know I didn't get your best season
and you didn't get mine
but maybe that was life's way of playing fairly.

Sugar Too Sweet

It was fun until the end
is that not but a cliché way to begin
of course, the end was my demise
never again would I hold you close
and ponder that look in your eyes
the gaze that held me steady in the night
through the ever-shifting dark times.

Alexandra Vincent

It seems as though the things
we need the most
can be the hardest to find
and the things that need to go
stay engraved in our minds.

Sugar Too Sweet

I thought I would miss you forever
the longing in my chest
would linger indefinitely
never giving my heart a rest

but now I see it's been
days
weeks
months
of joy well spent
not one moment wishing for you
or wondering where you went
the days of missing you reached the end
and now I realize

I can breathe again.

The dust finally settled
when my feet stopped circling
stopped chasing the moments
that have long passed
my mind can rest
among the cobwebs that grow
because my soul has been freed
and your heart I forego.

Sugar Too Sweet

Now I walk around in shaking shoes
watching everyone move
no longer a girl in the clouds
but a weed stuck in the ground
forever stagnant
in a world that's constantly moving.

Alexandra Vincent

Shame
leeches on you
and not the hottest of fires
could burn it away
they can see it on my face
I'm red with shame.

Sugar Too Sweet

A piece of my former self
still stung from the past
lives beneath the surface
unwell and unworthy she feels
a teenage melodrama stuck on repeat
but she tries so hard
to outrun the bees.

There comes a time
when self-respect is more dire
then a season of love.

Sugar Too Sweet

Lay your heart down

for the hurried beat can't bear no more.

Not everyone has the same heart
the special ones though
have golden honeycomb
that beats passionately
in their chest
and the love is pure and raw
dripping honey like a waterfall.

Sugar Too Sweet

The heart clung to new beginnings
and with time
love was reclaimed
and without fearing a love too sweet
the heart dripped with honey once again.

Dear reader,

Thank you for taking the time to sit with my words. I'm honored that my book can find a place in your home. Now that it's time to go back into the world, remember — it's okay to share your love. It's alright to open your heart to con-nection. Trust yourself.

With much love,

Alex

Find more of my work

Instagram - @alexandra.j.vincent
Tiktok - @alexandra.j.vincent
author website - alexandrajvincent.com

About the Author

Alexandra Vincent is an author who explores the vast human emotions and the healing process through poetry. She is the author of her debut poetry collection, *Monarch*. She wrote her second collection, *Sugar Too Sweet*, to share relatable thoughts and feelings from her personal story of love and loss. She shares her poetry with the hope of building a connection with her readers. When she's not writing poetry you will likely find her with her nose in a book, sipping chia tea, or chatting with any cat that crosses her path.

Ingram Content Group UK Ltd.
Milton Keynes UK
UKHW021432070623
423003UK00009B/66